Philosophical Fragments of a Contemporary Life

Philosophical Fragments of a Contemporary Life

Of a

Contemporary Life

Julien David

Upper West Side Philosophers, Inc.

New York   2008

CONTENTS

How to read this book / 13

~

The following aphorisms and essays on the most diverse subjects are not presented as truths but, rather, as snapshots of thinking intended to provoke thinking in turn and, at times, to entertain. They should be enjoyed, examined, tested, and falsified.

J. D.   *New York City*
                         October 2007

THE FRAGMENTS

Would it were possible to capture the world—
life, fate, human folly and human achievement—
the small and the big things, sadness, happiness,
childhood and old age, music, poetry, love,
friendship and hatred, and pain—in one long
aphorism!

(Marquis de Rossignol)

All men of whatever quality they be, who have
done anything of excellence, or which may prop-
erly resemble excellence, ought, if they are per-
sons of truth and honesty, to describe their life
with their own hand; but they ought not to at-
tempt so fine an enterprise till they have passed
the age of forty.

(Benvenuto Cellini)

Some say that thinking makes you sad. What nonsense! If anything, thinking makes you realize that what *makes* you sad is *you*. Thinking is a most effective and lasting remedy for sadness.

It is commonly held that lying is the opposite of telling the truth. Clearly, however, this cannot be the case, as it is possible not to tell the truth without lying at the same time. This misconception is based on the assumption that both lying and telling the truth belong to the same—declarative—category of speech. Lying and telling the truth are held to be two, diametrically opposed, modes of saying that something is or is not such and such, or that something is or is not the case. While this assumption is certainly correct, it makes us all too easily forget that what makes a statement a lie is not a function of its grammatical structure but of its intentional, volitional, or dispositional thrust. In other words, an untrue statement becomes a lie not because it is not true, but because it was said with the intention or will to deceive. Not telling or speaking the truth is not equal to lying.

What is important about this realization is that it allows us to make a categorical distinction between lying and truth, which may in turn have important consequences for the way we deal with the question of truth and lying in the various domains of our lives: Lying falls within the purview of ethics, the question of truth falls within the purview of metaphysics or ontology. Lying bespeaks a certain disposition, volition, or stance toward the world and oneself; truth pertains to the way the world and everything in it is or is not.

Thus, we can reasonably teach or expect a person not to lie, but we cannot, at bottom, expect a person to tell or speak the truth, as 'truth', being a metaphysical problem, will essentially remain undecided.

In philosophy the wheel must constantly be reinvented. Knowing what others have thought is not (yet) thinking.

Why the adage 'history teaches nothing' is and is not true

If we want to understand the significance of this much-invoked bit of proverbial wisdom we have to ask what 'teaches nothing' exactly means in this context. For, surely, it cannot simply mean what it says given that we can obviously learn, for instance, from past mistakes and hence from history, which is consequently capable of teaching us something. In order to make sense of this adage, then, we have to examine its underlying assumptions.

The first assumption is that history is, at bottom, a negative process marked by suffering and violence—hence, the implied injunction to learn from history so as to do it better in the future. The second assumption is that the same bad things continue happening without any real sign of improvement. In light of these assumptions 'teaches nothing' would seem to suggest that we are incapable, on the whole, of making the world better.

This holds true only if we think of history as a zero-sum game played out between victims and perpetrators, whereby both sides learn how 'better' to do what they do, with the perpetrators always being one step ahead of the victims, as it were. The perpetrators get better at inflicting harm, the victims get better at withstanding the perpetrators' onslaughts—but never quite good enough to be able to fend them off completely. The net result remains the same. Thus, only from the impersonal viewpoint of divine objectivity would it be true to say that 'history teaches nothing'. From the perspective of individual life, this statement can hardly be true, as we all can, and sometimes do learn from the past, which doesn't mean that we always know how to put what we have learned to good use.

ON ACADEMICS AND WHY THEY ARE DANGEROUS

Academics can be divided into four kinds: those in whom extreme intelligence is coupled with a sense of (extreme) superiority; those in whom intelligence is coupled with a sense of inferiority; those in whom stupidity is coupled with a sense of (extreme) superiority; and, finally, all those in between. (Those in whom stupidity is coupled with inferiority could never make it in the academy.)

Those of the first kind are dangerous because they typically know what they want and how to get it; those of the second kind are dangerous because they tend to act on emotion rather than reason; those of the third kind are dangerous because they will act at any scheming flatterer's bidding and because they don't tolerate competition and criticism; those of the fourth kind are dangerous because they would do anything to be counted among the first.

Most people are cowards. They will watch you put yourself on the line and wait to see what happens. If you win, they will rally behind you. If you lose, they will keep a distance. tance.

If we are lucky, our parents are, up to a certain point in our lives, our biggest supporters—the point at which we begin outgrowing them, thereby threatening the precarious equilibrium of their lives. If we are then lucky, they will not become our enemies.

~

Is friendship between parents and children possible? Friendship presupposes equality, and children and parents are never equals.

~

We owe our children everything and our parents nothing. To give ourselves to our children is an obligation, to give ourselves to our parents a gift.

~

It is particularly paralyzing to realize that we may not be able to save our children from themselves. We are at once both Protagoras and Socrates—hoping that virtue can be taught and suspecting that it can't.

Power only works in the face of fear. It loses its force as soon as it is met with indifference and courage.

~

Most of us are afraid of something most of the time.

On fear

Those who instill fear end up fearing those who fear them.

—with W. H. Auden in mind

A well-known philosopher has recently suggested that "bullshit is a greater enemy of the truth than lies are" because unlike lying, which recognizes the "authority of the truth" in the very act of rejecting it, bullshit does not reject the authority of truth but simply "pays no attention to it at all." Bullshit is "neither on the side of the true nor on the side of the false." Unlike the "honest man and the liar," the bullshitter is not concerned at all with facts or truth. To the extent that the "authority of the truth" is the very core and foundation of our society, consequently, the bullshitter can be said to pose a greater threat to it than the liar: Bullshitting "constitutes a more insidious threat than lying does to the conduct of civilized life," insofar as it is rooted in truth.

The logic underlying this argument can be formalized roughly as follows: Not paying any attention to x at all, or not being concerned with x at all—whereby x is to be understood as the core and foundation of y—is a greater threat to (the viability of) y than outrightly rejecting x. Or, to put it differently: Outrightly denying the validity of

x is a lesser threat to y than paying no attention to x at all.

On paper this may look like a sexy formula. In truth, however, this crude exercise in binary logic can easily be revealed as being itself a piece of 'bullshit' posing as a viable ethics. For, applied to real life, this argument would mean that those who pay no attention to us at all pose a greater threat to our life-world than those who explicitly reject us. On this logic, it would have been even worse for the Jews if the Nazis had paid no attention to them at all! What nonsense!

In the interest of survival, I suggest that we pay attention to those in particular who explicitly reject us and not worry about those who ignore us.

~

On a final note: Insofar as the bullshitter is as likely to say something that is true as something that is not true—having no grounds for choosing one or the other— shouldn't he be preferred to the (habitual) liar, who will, by definition, not tell the truth?

—in response to H. G. Frankfurt's *On Bullshit* (Princeton, 2005) and *Truth* (New York, 2006)

32

Your greatest enemies are those whom you have seen in a moment of shame and who know that you saw them. They will never forgive you for it.

We pay a high price for both not following love and following what we mistake for love. The price of the latter is nostalgia, the price of the former regret.

Even those who love you unconditionally have conditions—and they know it.

One of my favorite passages in philosophy is the following:

And so a gathering like this of ours, when it includes such men as most of us claim to be, requires no extraneous voices, not even of the poets, whom one cannot question on the sense of what they say; when they are adduced in discussion we are generally told by some that the poet thought so and so, and by others, something different, and they go on arguing about a matter which they are powerless to determine. No, this sort of meeting is avoided by men of culture, who prefer to converse directly with each other, and to use their own way of speech in putting one another by turns to the test. It is this sort of person that I think you and I ought rather to imitate.

~

We, academics, all too often hide behind the words of others—preferably, dead others—presuming to understand them "better than they understood themselves," as a critic once put it. If Socrates' final piece of advice to Alcibiades were to become the equivalent of the Hippocratic Oath for scholars in the humanities, our colleges and universities would

(can it hoped?) be staffed with fewer hyp-
ocrites ...

—in response to Plato's *Protagoras* 347e-348a

37

If you are free nobody can pressure you—
even under pressure the decision is yours.

Metaphor and metonymy are a blessing and a curse: a gift—perhaps the greatest—as without them we would not be able to communicate; and poison—perhaps the deadliest—because they empower us to draw a line between those who shall live and those who shall die.

On getting old

You first realize that you are getting old
when you begin feeling that you would like
to be young again.

In logic, a distinction is commonly made between analytic and synthetic judgments. Both kinds of judgment are concerned with the relation between subject and predicate. In the case of analytic judgments, the predicate is considered part of the very concept of the subject; in the case of synthetic judgments, the predicate is considered external to the concept of the subject. From this it follows that analytic judgments are by definition not based on experience, while all judgments of experience are by definition synthetic. Thus, as Immanuel Kant explains, "all bodies are extended" is an analytic judgment because the very concept of 'body' implies extension, whereas "all bodies are heavy" is a synthetic judgment because the concept of 'body' does not imply 'being heavy'—this, according to Kant, can only be known from experience.

In light of the distinction between synthetic and analytic judgments, the structure of prejudice can be described as follows: A prejudice is an unverified synthetic judgment posing as an analytic judgment.—All too often, we allow ourselves to be duped by this

logical masquerade—herein lies its perni-
ciousness.

When it comes to love, one of the most destructive things you can do is to demand the love that you are already receiving.

"Not even God himself can escape fate," the Delphic oracle is reported as saying to Croesus after his defeat by Cyrus.

Herodotus presents the story of the rise and fall of the Lydian empire under the Mermnadae, beginning with Gyges' usurpation of the throne and ending with the demise of his great-great-grandson, Croesus, at the hands of the Persians, as a cautionary tale about transgression and retribution: Gyges' crime—murdering king Candaules, stealing "his office, to which he had no claim," and marrying the queen—is decreed to be expiated in the fifth generation. The mode of expiation, as the Delphic oracle foretells Croesus, who misinterprets the prophecy, taking it to refer to the Persians, whom he is poised to attack: the destruction of a great empire—his own, as he is soon to find out.

~

Clicking the 'send' button and knowing, as you click it, that you shouldn't have sent the e-mail is as close as we come to experiening fate in the digital age …

—in response to Herodotus' *Histories*, book 1

The courage to want the other's pain without wanting it is as important as the courage to be true to oneself.

Marriage—a good marriage—is not work:
it works.

—with a widespread belief in mind

Only rarely, if at all, are we given the chance to change the course of our life: in the aftermath of a cataclysmic event, perhaps—or in those rare moments when life itself hits us like a tidal wave, flooding the shores of our being and hurling us into the truth of our future. Whether we choose to live by our truth, or whether we choose to betray it—there is no way back.

On being Jewish

What does it mean to be Jewish?—Depending on whom you talk to, being Jewish will be understood in racial, ethnic, national, cultural, or religious terms. Above all, however, being Jewish is a state of heart and mind.

The day when Martin Heidegger, president of the University of Freiburg, denied his teacher, Edmund Husserl, access to the university library because he was Jewish.

To the extent that we turn a blind eye to the misdeeds of others if we stand to benefit from them, we are all opportunists.

Those who are out to get you will always find a reason to find fault with what you do, no matter what you do. Trying to meet their expectations is utterly futile, as they expect you to fail one way or another.

Never complain to one spouse about the other, unless you want to lose the friendship of both.

Knowing where your responsibilities end is as important as knowing what you are responsible for.

—with Emmanuel Levinas in mind

On Kant's definition of enlightenment

Immanuel Kant defines enlightenment as our emergence from our self-imposed nonage. This implies that we must have already been enlightened before we imposed nonage on ourselves and, consequently, that the imposition of nonage on ourselves must have been an enlightened act. Why would we have given up being enlightened in the first place?

True dialogue is rare. More often than not, we talk *at* rather than *with* our interlocutors—what looks like dialogue is, in fact, bilateral monologue.

55

Love—whatever else it may be—is the realization that the other comes first.

I was driving our friend, Moishe Mandelbaum, to Grand Central Station that morning. "There's always an extra moron in the street for you," he said, as I was pulling up to the curb at Vanderbilt Avenue and David Ben-Gurion Place and almost bumped into the cab in front of us—"including yourself!" he added. "That's good!" I said—"that's really good—did you come up with it?" "Yes," he said, "a long time ago."

I retrieved his backpack from the trunk, we said our good-byes, and he walked off. How much life, I thought to myself, as I was watching this seventy-six-year old immigrant from Lithuania cross the street toward the Main Concourse, goes into a good aphorism!

Fairness is a tactical notion. What is and what is not considered fair depends on four factors: the situation, the parties involved, the framework of distributive justice in place, and those who have the power of decision. Because one can never be certain that the parties involved, or those who have the power of decision will be inclined toward fairness, it is fair to say that life is not fair.

The real reason why lawyers have a bad reputation is neither because they are greedy and cannot be trusted nor because the world would, presumably, be a less litigious and, hence, better place without them, but because we are too disingenuous not to impute our own greediness, litigiousness and mendacity to them. Our lawyers are as greedy, litigious and mendacious as we ask them to be on our behalf.

What makes a philosopher great is his capacity philosophically to conjure an entire new world, which we in turn must imagine ourselves inhabiting in order to determine whether we like or dislike his philosophy.

ON THE iPhone

so much depends
upon

a small dotted
- i -

beside the Book
the Mac

the Pod and
the Phone ...

... for it was made for you!

For J.-P. S.

It may take a lifetime to free oneself of the superstitious belief that one's name is one's destiny. Why should it be? How could it be? After all, destiny has to do with fate, and fate has to do with the gods, and chances are that the gods had nothing to do with your parents' decision to give you this or that name—giving names being a human affair, after all.

What would Rousseau have to say about this *faux* Geneva—more Stoic, more native, more tribal—were he to return and rewrite the *Social Contract*?

Here, at last, Seneca would have been per-
mitted to indulge his love for the emperor's
niece—a coarser, more rugged love—his
chin turned toward Rome, his heart moored
to Dresden, his grim future buried in Mos-
cow.

For D. G.

"Life is short, but art endures," they say. This is a false opposition, as art endures only to the extent that it has been infused with life. This means not only that art and life are never less than coterminous, but that, if anything, life outlives art and not the other way around.

More often than not, we don't gain anything by being right. In the best case, it is redundant—in the worst case, it makes us look self-righteous and arrogant. Often, being wrong is preferable to being right—at least we can learn something from it.

Often, when we say "I didn't mean it" we are disingenuous, for we did mean to say what we now say we didn't mean when we said it. Often, "I didn't mean it" really means "I wish I hadn't meant it."

A friend not only wants you to be well and do well, but he is actually happy with you when you are doing well.

~

It is often easier to offer sympathy and support to a friend in need than to celebrate a friend's prosperity and successes without envy.

~

Like love, friendship is not based on need.

Genuine novelty is rare. Most of the time, novelty means that we have forgotten to remember that in one way or another it has been said or done before.

Aristotle's metaphysics, Descartes' method of doubt, Edmund Husserl's logic, Emmanuel Levinas' ethics—all self-proclaimed *First Philosophies*. Which one, now, is actually first?

> —in response to Descartes' silent debt to Aristotle's *Metaphysics* 1005b-1006a, 1011a-b

"Efface the thought, I am harmed, and at once the feeling of being harmed disappears; efface the feeling and the harm disappears at once."
    (Marcus Aurelius, *Meditations*, book 4, 7)

For Marshall B. Rosenberg

The memory of a promise in the future perfect.

On revenge, *more cynico*

When asked how one should avenge oneself on one's enemies, Diogenes replied: by behaving like a gentleman. Similarly, Marcus Aurelius advised that the best way of avenging oneself is not to do likewise.

~

Harboring thoughts of revenge poisons your life. The unexpected gift of revenge undesired is sweet.

On genius

Genius, J. W. Goethe once said, is the power to compel a critic to alter his judgment.

~

When I think of genius, I think of the ocean: breakers leaving no marks, small waves pleasant to behold and dip into, tall waves that challenge without threat, tidal waves that destroy and remake—stormy at times, and calm—unpredictable, always, and always a temptation.

Recently, my teenage son began writing aphorisms. One, in particular, strikes me as a perfect exemplar of the genre: "Often, when an adult underestimates a child's intelligence, he actually overestimates his own."

Philosopher, literary critic, and translator Julien David, whose real name is Michael Eskin, was educated at the University of Munich, the Institut Catholique de Paris, Concordia College, and Rutgers University. A former fellow of Sidney Sussex College, Cambridge, he has taught at the University of Cambridge and at Columbia University, and is the cofounder of Upper West Side Philosophers, Inc., and the Independent Center for Philosophical Thinking in New York City. He has published widely on literary and philosophical subjects, including *Nabokov's Version of Pushkin's "Eugene Onegin": Between Version and Fiction—a Study in Translation and Fiction Theory* (Sagner 1994); *Ethics and Dialogue in the Works of Levinas, Bakhtin, Mandel'shtam, and Celan* (Oxford University Press 2000); *Literature and Ethics: A Special Edition of Poetics Today* (Duke University Press 2004); and *Poetic Affairs: Celan, Grünbein, Brodsky* (Stanford University Press 2008). *Philosophical Fragments of a Contemporary Life* is Michael Eskin's first publication under the pen name Julien David. He lives in New York City with his wife and three sons.

Published by Upper West Side Philosophers, Inc., P. O. Box 250645, New York, NY 10025.

The colophon is a registered trademark of Upper West Side Philosophers, Inc.

Library of Congress Control Number: 2007937372
ISBN-13: 978-0-9795829-2-9
ISBN-10: 0 9795829-2-X

Design: Upper West Side Philosophers, Inc.
Printed by Offset Impressions, Inc., Reading, PA
Printed in the United States of America